Paddling through the Meridian's Wake

poems by

Greg Maddigan

Finishing Line Press
Georgetown, Kentucky

Paddling through the Meridian's Wake

ACKNOWLEDGMENTS

Thank you very much to my children, Abigail, Evelyn, Patrick, and Isabelle, for
being first readers and listeners for many of the poems in *Paddling through the
Meridian's Wake*. Your suggestions were invaluable. Mom and Dad, thank you
for making all of these wild synapses possible. Thank you also to Ginny Lathem
for her willingness to accept a poem every year for her birthday. Joan Schwab, I
am so grateful for the gift of piano music in the background while I edit. Mike,
Coley, and Mary Anne, thank you for putting up with all of the random poetry
over the years and for your constant affirmation. David Shea, as always, thank
you for being the keeper of the file. Thank you to my beautiful wife Stacy for
being my prime meridian. Finally, thank you readers, for spending some time
Paddling through the Meridian's Wake. All mistakes are mine.

Editor: Christen Kincaid

Cover Art: Abigail Maddigan

Author Photo: Isabelle Maddigan

Cover Design: Elizabeth Maines

Printed in the USA on acid-free paper.
Order online: www.finishinglinepress.com
also available on amazon.com

Author inquiries and mail orders:
Finishing Line Press
P. O. Box 1626
Georgetown, Kentucky 40324
U. S. A.

Table of Contents

For Stacy

In Canoes

At sunset,
we fish
the long curve of the river,
the one that bends like the arc of our lives.
We can't remember what lies
ahead or behind.
We watch the fish
rise and ripple
the surface
like meditations.
They brush the edges
of their watery confines,
chasing lures, then cower
at the shadows thrown by Ospreys
circling in another world.
We cast our spools of shimmering light
again and again
into uncertainty,
Longing for the catch,
Longing to be present when the two worlds converge,
Longing to leave our canoes and walk on water.
Soon, the sun will vanish
Behind the mountains.
We paddle through the meridian's wake.
In the darkness,
in our dreams,
we will hear the eternal current
lapping against our hulls.
If only we could
walk on water.

The Big Bang

You stand on the
Bottom stair
In your red cowgirl boots
With the January light
Shattering on the street
Around you
Like blue lake ice,
Like my middle-aged
Passion,
Another false promise about
Slow-moving time.
You beckon me
With your curling finger,
Towards the sapphire
Orb
Dangling on your sternum.
I wait
For your lips
To part and reveal
My impetus—
Words, only for me,
Spinning from your mouth
Like the Big Bang.
If only we could move
Together
Towards Death, like this light,
Like glaciers
Immovable in their churned up moraines.

Driving Down the Gorge

We are wistful in the evening
As we watch the West pass by our windows.
Coal cars clack alongside irrigated farms,
Chasing the orange crescent of today's remains.

The land wears the trains
Like necklaces—
Little beads blackened by our collective desires.

Dark blue pools rest on the scablands
Like vestigial gardens
Inviting the skittish elk out of their hideaways.

We roll the windows down.
The summer air,
Thick with reminiscence
And the smell of the harvest,
Rustles our senses.
We wish we could drive forever.

Red-Tailed Hawks
Sit stoically on the power poles
Like purveyors of the dwindling electrons of eternity,
Oblivious to our electric minds.

The fishermen check their set nets
On the bend in the Columbia
And sit and jostle and parse
The minuscule details of the day
Waiting for meaning.

We savor it all,
Infatuated with the pressing transience,
While aching for permanence.
We try to grasp
The rain light falling through the far-off ceiling of sky
Like grace, unasked for, essential and elusive.
We marvel at
The white capped waterway in this Gorge,
The blue-green river, darkened by dusk,
surging at the foot of the raucous and wild forests,
Bounding beneath the wind-bent trees
Like a pulse,
Endlessly spilling itself onto the battered driftwood beaches of the
wide Pacific.

The waters wend their way into history, into the coming swells,
into the coming days,
The ones we long for but know we will never see.

There are no words
Good enough
For all of this.

But words are all we have
And they will have to do:

The rain draping across the valley
The Sharp-Shinned Hawk perched on his crumbling column of
basalt and belief
The still covered Cascades lying in the distance like adolescent
memories
Reluctant to be forgotten.

The way your bronzed skin wears the light like amber jewelry,
The way your green eyes capture the color of the
Continental Divide emptying itself down deep
Channels, full of torrential import.

We long to catch these moments,
To pin them down.
But when we try,
They turn to ash in our fingers.

We wonder at the goodness of it all,
At whether it has been a hoax.
We wonder if living selflessly or selfishly ultimately
Changes the nature of reality.

We catapult backwards into the present
Where critical minds cringe at sentimentality
Where windmills shudder on the bluffs at sunset
Where closed minds cringe at tolerance
Where dams thunder with abundance
Where our logic deteriorates like television snow
Falling on the wind-swept steppes and tumbleweed towns
Of Americana.

At last, we know, the gold hills above the vineyards make promises
They won't be able to keep.

We cling to this glistening orb
Like fuzz to a peach
Like continents to some ancient, foundational
Pangaea
Like rain droplets to conifer needles
Like ridiculous hope.

We can no longer think in prose.
The words come only in
Disjointed spots of poetry and incoherence,
The words we wish our fathers and brothers, our mothers and sisters,
Our sons and daughters,
Could try to understand,
But the words are only for us, for our long sojourn into the way
things really are.

If only eternity were riding with us in the backseat.

Maybe we could pretend for a bit longer.

Sundays, Too

On Sundays, too,
We go to the woods.

We launch our canoe
Into the emerald waters
Sending ripples across the stillness
Like mumbled prayers.
We paddle with reverence
Crossing again and again
From port to starboard
Emerging into this new watery world.
We are bathed in morning's white light,
Where we can finally, unfortunately, see ourselves clearly.
We clutch our wooden paddles like umbilical cords
Or the weather-worn crooks of our fathers.

We drift below Jake's Mountain,
The red cliffs set in the blue buttress of sky
Like stained glass.
Suddenly, eagles, three of them, glide overhead,
Circling like the merry-go-rounds of childhood,
The ones we couldn't quite quit.
Above us, wings spin dizzyingly, swirling like
The chaotic words of our subconscious.
Closer now, the eagles descend to the water,
Their feathers flapping like
Tibetan prayer flags,
Like exquisite kites
In too much wind,
Waiting to be reeled in
On the taut strings of belief.

They rise again on the faith
Of air currents, unlike us,
Never doubting what they can't see,
Keeling and chirping
Like our secret hearts,
Up, up
Until one swoops down,
Talons in the water
And lifts off again
With a wriggling
fish,
In its final moments,
Bright-speckled and brilliant,
Like we wish we could be.
It's what we long for.

The eagles disappear
Into the chanting forest.
We gaze at each other, convinced
That just beneath the marrow and carbon
Of all things
Lies eternity.

On Sundays, too,
What choice do we have, but to
Go to the woods.

Wheat in Winter

With you, my wife,
In late November,
While driving two lane roads
Which wind and unwind like the
Blue veins
In our hands,
We see
        Wheat in winter
            Surging upward
               Surging green
Everywhere horizons of green
180 degrees of impossibility.
Like your eyes, I say.

These Thanksgiving skies
Watery blue, old color
Diluted like our desires,
Diluted like
God shrugged,
Unimpressed with our
Vibrancy
Our distant trysts, unwilling to
Make a world that matched
The fire of our minds.
We silently long
For the far-gone,
Our tinder-box youth,
The swell of summer, curving like
Your body in the
Golden light, the long smooth
Legs of memory,
Of days lounging under solar flares

Of wheat bristling in the
Undulating fields, the Palouse
Hills rising and falling
With my heart.

And
Who could dismiss
The Red barn
Where we once met, where we
Might meet again?
In the car, I squeeze your hand—
The splintered door swings
Slightly inward.
Cats laze in the rafters.
Dust beams defy gravity—
They float improbably,
Like galaxies, like souls,
Like we once believed we could,
We would.

In the hay loft
We listened for voices
Beyond the whispering husks,
But heard only the sound
Of invisible comets rushing away
From us.
From the high window
We watched the
Combine roll towards fall
Bringing in sweat and joy
Bushel by bushel
Rolling through row after row
Of possibilities, for you,

And for me
Stolen glances
At the glories sealed in the
Ball jars of youth.
We only wanted
To remain there forever
And over and over again.
We never knew enough,
Never thought to consider
Anticipating the shortened days
And the possibility of, the
Necessity of
Fallow fields and
Never again.

And so we look and look again,
All around us,
The fleeting
Brilliant green
Of winter wheat.
Like your eyes, I say.
You squeeze my hand
And we drive
Into
The coming evening.

bottled up

I stopped by the Chevron
At the corner of Main Street and
The wilderness
To get propane for the grill.
Old Haines trundled out,
Roused by the bell,
His gait belying his age.
His barrel chest was like
A rusted bird cage
Swinging in the dusk,
Housing an electric canary.
"You want energy?" he asked, taking my empty.
I nodded. Didn't we all?
"Don't make the big mistake," he said,
Deftly rigging the nozzle.
"What's that?" I asked.
"Filling it too full," he said.

He nodded up towards the sheer face
Of Scotchman Peak, seven thousand feet of rising
Wonder, brown rock wall checkered white with snow, as if
The mountain were explanation enough.
The propane tank expelled a sigh, a white puff of gas that
Obscured his screwdriver.
Filling it too full?
Too late, I thought.

In my mind, I saw the
Cedar trees, uncut, unbucked, uprooted by the winter storms and
Tossed by the current
Of Lightning Creek, the raucous pockets of white
Bucking my sense of order,
Of divinity. The water surged above the banks,
Above the dignity of
Rules, of propriety, of morality, of mortality:

Wild,
Flowing like the wine at Cana
Like my unspoken thoughts, my mute-mouthed finger-beading
prayers.
Too late, I thought.

I saw the Red-winged Blackbird
A lone voice, swaying on the dried cattails,
Preparing at least two nests,
Covering his bets, preparing for rejection, for failure,
His instinct knowing that nature would love to serve his head on a
platter.
Too late.

I sat with my brothers and sisters at table,
Dipping bread and eating, retreating
Into our cavernous souls, bone-weary,
Waiting for a nap in the garden, wishing for a prayer carpet,
Knowing doubt, knowing we would eventually have to
Dip our fingertips into the oozing stigmata.
And the stars spin infinitely on their loom,
Rising again and again
Above the Gethsemane of our lives:
Wild, like swirling thickets of thorns, dervishes of
Self-sacrifice.
Too late.

I saw the Robins in the matted grasses,
Ubiquitous, worrying over worms,
Like April farmers worrying over their sometimes soon-to-be futile
scratchings,
Their fields unrolling towards the horizon like ancient scrolls,
Worrying wildly
Like all of us.
Too late.

I saw the Herons,
With the stillness of monks,
Furtive
The color of dawn,
Beaks like scissors, seeking,
Hunting
In the water which glinted like silver dollars
Beneath the peach-colored clouds
The size of the Galapagos,
The size of mercy:
Wild.

I saw the Gold Finch at the pinnacle
Of the Ponderosa Pine,
Wearing his yellow vestments,
Singing his harmonic song
Of sex, of competition, of aggression,
Of sacred tradition, of doctrine, of wisdom:
Wild,
Never suspecting that his bones had been
Hollowed out by time and evolution.
How would he know? How would I know?
Beauty will not be undermined.
Too late.

I saw the Coots, the Mallards, the Buffleheads, the Cinnamon Teals,
The flapping-winged frenzy
On the slough, casting a curtain
Of chaos, like incense, like my midnight thoughts, my Triduum
prayers,
Across the fertile shadowy waters:
Wild,

Like my soul, our souls
Punctured by the branches and needles
Of the stout-poled pines on the hillside.

Back to the now, beside the big white whirring tank,
Near the breathing forests:
"4.5 out of 5 gallons," Old Haines said.
"Just to be safe."
He handed me the tank,
Heavy with all that we had bottled up in there.
Yes, I thought. Just to be safe.
If only.

Eastbound

This morning, in late October,
I drive east,
Rising up, through dark forests,
Into the white squall
Of Snoqualmie Pass.
I think
      I can
            feel
The unknown matter
Of the universe
Pressing in on my certainty.

Storm-narrowed highway, lines obscured,
My paradigm
Blurred,
Windows streaked
With chaos, with ancient water,
With the electromagnetic past.

Rising elevation, and the flakes fast-forward on the
windshield,
Like hyperspeed—
My arms strain
To hold the wheel, to control
The tires spinning in the ruts,
Strain like the tree boughs
Under the heavy new snow,
Strain to hold, strain to cling to
The primitive
Rites of my tribe.

What am I afraid of?
That I don't know what dark energy is.
That I can't comprehend sliding off this mountain,

Riding a light wave until
My headlights blink out in a broken, branch-snapped gully.
That my body, my particles, my
Ancient stardust will go on
Without me.

What am I afraid of?
That this old dispensation
Has crumbled
Again.
That I never understood gravity.
That the sun is not a burning bush.
That the universe is steadily
Abandoning us
And the wistful heartache of
Wishing that it wouldn't,
Wishing Copernicus had been wrong,
Wishing the Pope had locked Galileo up without his
instruments,
Wishing we could still be the center of it all.
Couldn't we all agree to allow our omniscient hubris
To remain unchecked? To be right because we
Firmly believe we are.

What am I afraid of?
That I don't know, can't know
The comforting curvature of the
Quilt of space-time.
That a parallel me exists in a
Plane where I can only cast stones
Into a timeless river while sitting
Near an impotent Siddhartha.
That Hemingway was faking his Catholicism.
That I only exist as a bit

On the face of a black hole.
That I should be focusing more
On my fish-tailing car than
On my existential concerns.

What am I afraid of?
That I'm no more important
Than a butterfly.

Now,
Over the summit,
I follow the red and gold trees
Along the river
Into the misty
Translucent
Dawn.
The ground is cold and hard with
Frost,
And I drive
At 186,000 miles a second
Towards home
Certain of the dead corn stalks in the fields,
Certain of the incense of the cows,
Certain of the rime on the veins of the fallen leaves,
Certain of the absence of the robins in the fallow pews
Of this Sunday morning,
Certain of the memory of a little boy
Playing mandolin on Pike Street,
The smell of fish and bread in the salty air, the crying gulls,
Certain that the Water Towers will beckon old farm pickups
To dusty intersections, crossroads of gab and gall
Certain of the stooped-back workers' summer-time return to the fields,
Certain that I could stop

And sit or stand or kneel
With my head covered or not,
And savor
The doctrine of the seasons,
The necessity of love,
The orchestra of dogs barking,
The divinity of grapes, clusters of succulent sadness hanging from
our hearts.
I am certain of the sun now streaming through the remnant clouds
As through stained glass,
Certain of my celestial skin enveloping my celestial bones,
Certain of my return home, to the smell of my daughter's pumpkin
bread
Cooking in the kitchen.

A Miracle

We leave the city,
Where on interstate ramps
The ragtag armies assemble
waving their hand-lettered cardboard signs
Like rifles
With their threatening smiles
Chiseled into craggy faces
Weathered by loss,
Shoving their grief down our throats
Their alms palms stretched out like vines of poison ivy.
We leave the city
Where broken families litter neighborhoods
Like junked out cars slumping in the heat,
Upholstery sprung and torn,
Tires flattened by cobwebs and dry grass
And the shatterproof glass of idealism,
Where dreams grow
Like weeds in the splintered cracks of asphalt.
The things poverty obliterates.
We are weary of kidding ourselves
That it could be different.

We leave the city
Where we have been trying to teach
Them
Teach the blind to see,
Teach the lame to walk,
Teach them how to walk on water.
We have been trying to teach
Them
To cherish themselves.
Maybe nobody else has.
Trying with only some avail.
We are weary.

We leave the city and go to the woods,
Take the long drive into the cool green
Forests, to the little cabin
In the tall trees.
Here
The empty knocking of a
Woodpecker's beak
On distant bark
Echoes the sound of our despair,
Our frustration at not being able to fix everything, anything.
The vibrations of the
Hummingbird's wings
Dull our longing for justice.
They zoom to and from the
Red feeder in the pre-dawn light,
Pumping life at a pace
We will never know.

We drink coffee
On the back deck
At the base of the big trees
And wonder at our brokenness
While the Nuthatches flit above
Unseen in the golden canopy of morning.

In the afternoons
We contemplate the innocence of children,
As ours slip through the forest unnoticed,
Slinging the arrows of their imaginations unbound.
We watch the turkeys
Usher their brood to the top of the rock
Behind the cabin, whooping and scratching
And finally flinging themselves
Unceremoniously
Into the high branches of simply making it another day.

We carry our inner disfigurement to the river
Where we let our shame at having failed
Float with us, past
The banks, the long sipping grasses,
The alders teeming with Tanagers,
Spotted Towhees, and Yellow Warblers.
We round a bend and surprise a
Heron, and hear his prehistoric croaking.
We watch him swing the long blade of his beak
Towards the sky,
Eternity whispering just beneath his wings
As he flaps away from us.

We think briefly of the city and wonder:
Is it giving up to think
that we can only do so much?
Now are we bruised cynics?

We watch a summer storm
Tumble up the lake, ricocheting off the edges
Like middle-aged anger.
It topples trees, uprooting them,
Snaps the giant cottonwoods in two,
Rains detritus down
On every open space,
Darkening cabins, dampening enthusiasm.
Some of us have no power to lose.

In the woods, we paddle beneath
The red lichen cliffs
Watching the eagles
Circle above us like pieces of a broken watch,
Unwinding time, unwinding our heads and hearts.
They perch in the towering trees,

Gazing down upon our flaws, our significance.
One swoops low,
Talons flashing, nearly anointing our foreheads,
And if we could, we would
retreat to the old cave, the old fire,
The old comforting rites.

We think,
What can we do but this, again and again,
And love?

We realize
The city is entwined in our gristle, it marbles our make up—
We can not escape it, nor should we try.

Where the river meets the lake
The wind moves on the open water
Like our first breath, like the prime mover.
The white caps are in a frenzy,
All moving towards the mountains, going nowhere.
The chiseled green waters pound the beach,
Beating the round rocks flat
Beneath the Green Monarchs.
The waves roll and unroll
Like scrolls of wisdom,
Shifting the rocks,
Overcoming the constancy of
The voices in our heads
Rattling and chattering with the back and forth of
All the years of human history,
The petitioning and listening,
Joining together with all the voices chanting, chanting:
We can only do the best with what we have.

It turns out
The city
Them
Is Us.
It turns out
We all long for mercy,
To be cherished,
To see, to walk, to improbably walk on water.
We all need a miracle.

Now while driving, with the wheels
Going round and round,
We return to the city,
Back to our work, our toil, our meaning.
We know we have glimpsed
Genesis, Eden
And we believe we can carry
Some sliver of it back with us.
We long to share it
And we refuse to relinquish it.

Perched

We heard it before we saw it.
My son's eleven year-old ears sensed
The wings,
The mysterious whispering:
Seemingly of something distant,
Something regal,
Something lost.
The owl—Great-Horned or Barred or Barn or Screech—
We didn't know which,
Carved the dusk
Above the lackluster campfire
Like a scythe in a sunset field of
Century-old wheat.
He glided into the old snag behind the camp,
Settling softly,
Just outside domesticity.
We stirred from our chairs
To the edge of the woods,
Unfettered from worry, single-minded, pursuing our quarry.

And then, perched on a scraggly branch that scratched
At evening and eternity,
He showed us his visage,
And unsettled my soul,
With his head spinning like a weathervane,
Unmoored from bone,
Hiding his mind, his intentions.
His eyes were clocks,
One telling time, the other telling dreams,
A squirming juxtaposition.
We watched his silence,
Back-dropped by the burgeoning stars,
Their apostolic radiance
Streaming through the liquid dark,

Chanting their incantations, their creeds,
Pressing their old light
Like glinting knives
Into my son's clear eyes, my weary pupils.

We stood immobile,
Star-struck by his omniscience,
Exhilarated
By his apathy,
His unutterable disinterest in our
Presence.
He hooted…who are you?

Blood and carbon, consecrated by 13.4 billion year-old
Stardust.
Who are you?

At last, he flapped away, above this Eden,
Into the wasteland
Of night and predation,
Of living and dying,
Of electric discharges,
Of energy ricocheting into the vast emptiness.
We hurried back to our fire,
Glad for the flickering exhaustion of atoms,
Glad for the tidy rocks,
The comfort of tradition.
My son was exuberant about his spotting, his find,
Eager to share his wonder, his questions.
But I cannot talk, cannot explain. I can only sit
With the shifting tectonics of my awe,
With the knowledge
That this spotting might be my last—
That now, in the chapel of my soul,
Things might never be the same again.

This Road

This road, you know the one,
The two lanes curving
Into your past,
Riding in the station wagon,
When your eyes just cleared
The sill and you could barely
Wrap your whole hand around
The knob and crank it,
Round and round
To roll the window down,
To let the wind romp in the back
Over your mother's objections
From the front.

You know the road,
The one from that time
When your parents were still
Together,
When you still thumb-wrestled your brother,
Still split a soda,
When chaotic laughter was a part of
Every single day.

You know the road,
The one with the tall trees,
The sequined lights of the oil rigs,
The smell of the sea,
The crowded chowder fog,
The road where your dad packs
The back with sleeping bags, a cooler, and
A propane lantern which will hiss
Like the Sirens to the fluttering and haphazard night moths.

Here, on this road,
There is a breeze.
It smells of the kelp beds
And the stellar gases
And the tar sands.
You coast closer to the end
And the anxiety rises, you worry that
Spot number 23 might already be taken,
Or that you might not get a spot at all,
Or that your brother will puke, and your mom will say,
"I knew he shouldn't have had that soda."
Or that some unforeseen hurdle
Will present itself and end your trip abruptly,
Like a sudden nosebleed, like your childhood.
And moreover, you worry that it
Will all end:
These trips with the broken down car
And the shimmying trailer
And the overheating radiator,
The reassuring nature of their voices alternating between
Giddy and tense,
Their love,
The simple foundation of your consciousness.

But this road leads to the place
Where mom and dad wear their
Matching blue camping jackets
With the synchronous swishing sound,
As if they wished for the same things, would always wish for the
same things:
For their future, their promise—your future, your promise—
All the same.
They walk the campground
Hand in hand,

While the pretty girl from
The next camp over plays tag with you
Past purple twilight.

Later, you burrow down
Against the damp cold, listening to talk of
Mars and Venus, of
I'm okay, You're okay, of
The big-hard-rock-candy mountain, of
Incomprehensible syllables.
You burrow down with
The blossomed joy, against
The burgeoning hurt,
Against overhearing too much,
The childish sounds of love,
While the night winds buffet the canvas.
Meanwhile, the sound of the surf
Shoving against the rocks
Will rise and rise and rise until
You ask your dad to check outside the trailer,
To reassure you that
The frothy, voracious tide
Has not breached the rocky seawall.
And once he has declared that all is safe,
The night becomes a time of hope,
Of deep breathing and rhythmic snoring for some,
And mania for others,
Of train whistles in the dark,
The Starlight run from Los Angeles
To San Francisco, flattening pennies
On the tracks of your beliefs.
This is the time of knowledge,
Breaking like the mysterious symmetry
Of the waves, in slow motion,

Time-lapsed and lingering
In the moonlight, rolling in from
The deep, the exotic.

Later, we realize that the road in is different
From the road out.
In the dark, we glimpsed
The bipolarity of existence, of God's Eden
And the slithering duplicity of free will,
As if either could exist in such simplicity.
We foretold our self-concern,
Our altruism, narcissism, and radiance,
and the tremulous beauty of our intelligence,
Exploring only the bright corners of this
Divine universe, since we could not, can not
See
In the dark.

The road out is different from
The road in,
And on the road out, there she is,
Later, much later, there she is,
In the yearning dusk,
In the wavering light,
Her wine-dark hair moving like
The ocean at sunset.
There she is,
Eyes glittering green
Like the bay,
Sparkling with phosphorescence,
The color of mirth, the color of wisdom,
The color of trying to do it differently,
Trying to last longer than human
Desires, human frailty,

Longer than the seasons,
The eruption of the pink cherry blossoms,
The yellow pine sperm on the windshield,
The unique crystals frozen to her sweeping tresses,
Longer than the burnished colors of death,
The frozen breath all around her,
Longer than the words
Evaporating in the confessional,
Longer than a lightning bug's feverish declaration
Of love,
Longer than the juice of a peach.

The road out comes with the realization that
It wasn't entirely their fault,
Swishing along in their blue jackets,
That they were part of a larger mosaic,
Evergreens in the fog, owls in the night, the big blue
Habitually orbiting, in Jupiter's shadow, 93 million miles from
Self-immolation,
The pale blue dot,
Rushing
To collide with the next galaxy, rushing in an
ever-expanding
          ever-accelerating
                    ever-darkening universe
Rushing.

It is hard to lay blame...
For the stars in their rotations,
For human hearts pumping
Nativism and universalism,
For winter's Orion, shooting misguided arrows of certainty,
For summer's vague constellations,
For the capricious nature of emotion,

For the wild flare of a meteor galloping towards the
Waiting desert,
For loving only what loves us back,
For loving only what is right in front of our
Gouged-out eyes,
For our ironies,
For the dirt, the worms,
The memories which will
Hopefully
Live as long as the written word
Engraved upon our headstones.

So now, what do we know?
Only of this road, the ins and outs,
The salt and the gulls and the riptides and the fires that won't start,
The Milky Way spread before us
Like a banquet of midnight grunion,
Only of this road,
Double-yellow lines, winding away from the past,
Towards more and more of the inescapable anxiety,
Towards the sighs of the long grasses in the dunes,
The waves rolling under the piers of indifference,
The flickering streetlamps of ambition,
The bright Ferris wheels of desire,
The soft comfort of earlobes,
The lovely chafing of sand in our sandals, the neck's nape,
The sacred tolling of the mission bells,
Of my fingers entwined with yours,
Of doing
The best
We can,
Just like they did.

Greg Maddigan attended Gonzaga University where he earned bachelor's degrees in English and Theology. Greg lives in Spokane, Washington with his wife, Stacy, and their four children. He teaches at the On Track Academy and spends his summers living and writing in a little cabin in the Lake Pend Oreille Country. Greg is also the author of the novel *Morning Gravity*. Greg has published his poetry in *The Legendary* literary magazine. *Paddling through the Meridian's Wake* is Greg's first publication of a collection of poetry by a literary press.

www.ingramcontent.com/pod-product-compliance
Lightning Source LLC
LaVergne TN
LVHW091234080426
835509LV00009B/1272